Projects in Leath

Camouflage

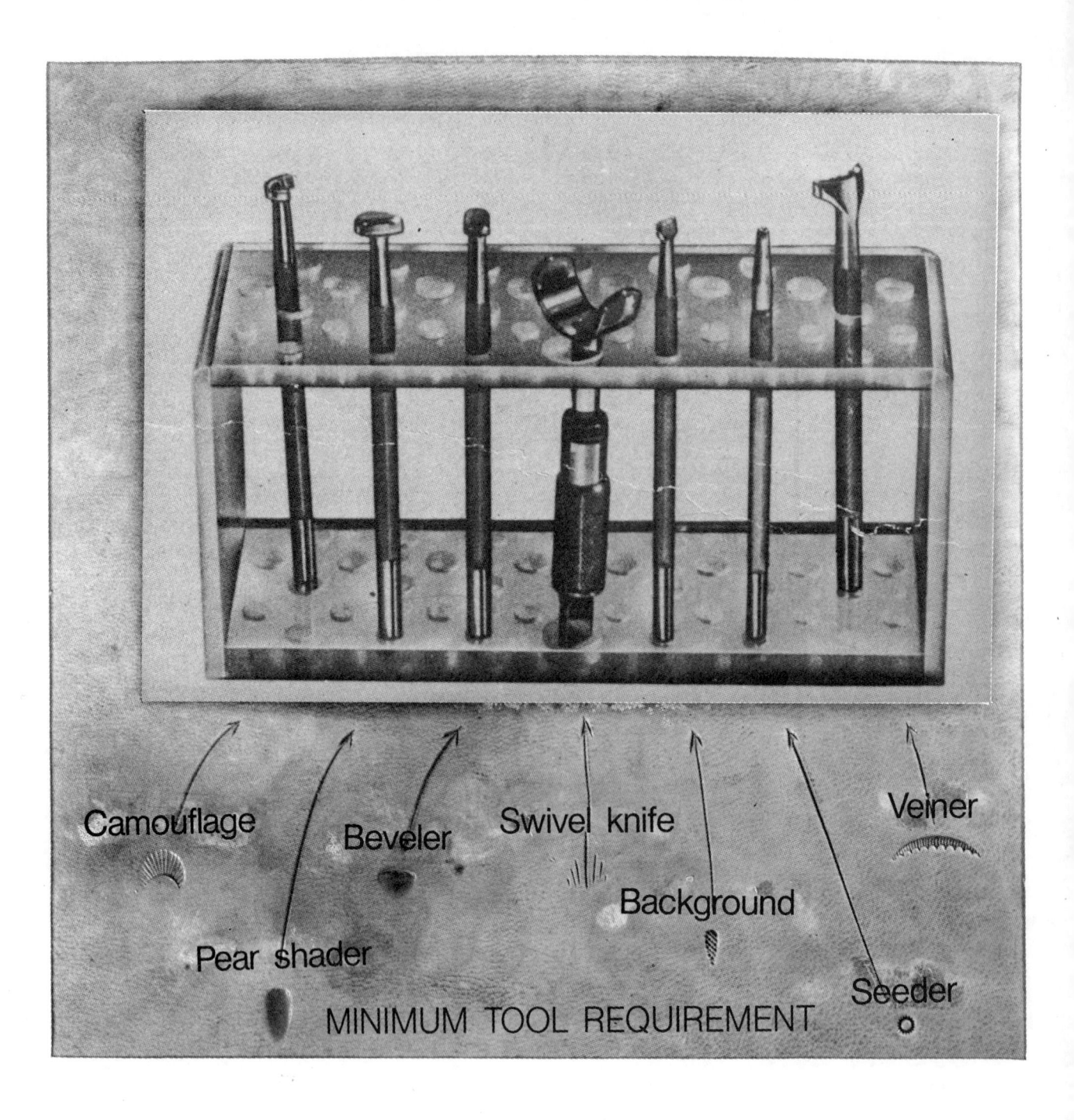

Beveler

Swivel knife

Background

Veiner

Pear shader

Seeder

MINIMUM TOOL REQUIREMENT

Projects in
LEATHER

Thor Kristinsson

Kangaroo Press

Photographs by R.V.J. Salter

© Thor Kristinsson 1985

Reprinted 1989
First published in 1985 by Kangaroo Press Pty Ltd
3 Whitehall Road (P.O. Box 75) Kenthurst 2156
Printed in Singapore by Singapore National Printers Ltd

ISBN 0-86417-016-5

Contents

Minimum tool requirement	ii
Getting started	vi
Brief history of leathercraft	1
Use of the basic tools	23
How to reduce or enlarge design	24
Leather thickness and use	25
Lacing requirements	26

Leather projects

Book markers	29
Coasters	30
Comb cases	31
Scissor cases	32
Coffee cup holders	35
Glasses cases	38
Wallets	42
Pocket secretary	68
Belts	77
Lady's hats	85
Photo frames	87
Cheque book cover	100
Magazine binding	106
Book cover	110
Photo albums	113

Balsawood–leather projects

Introduction	121
Letter holder	125
Book ends	130
Cigarette box	135
Cuckoo watch	139
Table lamp	143

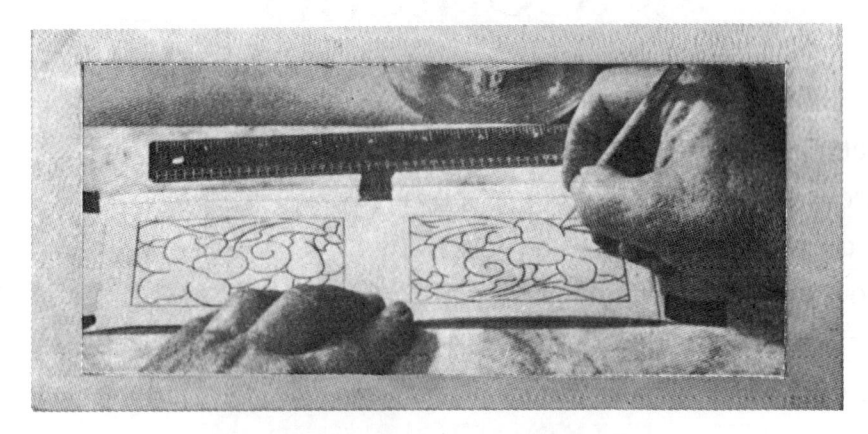

Tracing the design on the leather

Moisten the leather

Holding the tools

GETTING STARTED

Brief history of leathercraft.

The decorating of leather is one of the most intriguing, as well as ancient, teachings in the history of mankind. To trace the history of leather and leathercraft through the ages is as interesting as to practise the craft. In light of this fact it is surprising indeed to find so many people not acquainted with the history and romance of leather. This becomes even more surprising when we consider that there is scarcely a teacher of the craft that has not been asked at some time in their teaching career, "When did leathercraft begin?"

To answer this question with the simple statement, "In the beginning" is by no means an attempt to be facetious.

In Biblical times man first began to use leather through necessity. According to the Bible (Genesis 3:21) "Unto Adam and also unto his wife did the Lord God make coats of skins and clothed them."

We also learn through the findings of the anthropologists, that the cavemen were clothed in hides of furbearing animals. While there is no definite evidence, there is very little possibility that there was much decorative art or carving on leather at that time. There were no suitable tools with which to work leather.

The only tool available was a piece of flint, chipped to provide a scraping edge.

Documentary evidence of the beginning of the craft is vague and sketchy. A thirteenth century manuscript shows a crude drawing of a bovine being slaughtered and it is presumed- in the manuscript- that the hide was to be converted into leather and put to use in any of the then-limited ways the material was used.

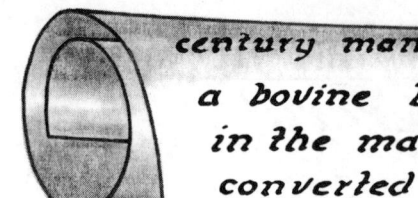

Leather with or without the fur on it undoubtedly was a factor in the survival of early man. This was definitely true of the great ice age.

In all probability the only method of treating hides in those days was the rubbing of the dried hides thoroughly with the brains and fat of the animal until they were "cured" or at least were made more pliable.

Another method was chewing the leather until it was softer and more supple. This method was practised extensively by the American Indians and is today still done by Eskimo women. So, leather thus treated was used in early times for shoes (moccasins), garments shelter and other necessities.

As civilization progressed and as the art became more advanced man began decorating leather by adding metal trimming such as silver mountings, by dyeing and by carving and stamping. Some definite documentary evidence does exist from about the eleventh century. It was written in Aelfric's Colloquies that." I buy my hides and skins and prepare them by my craft and I make of them boots of various kinds, ankle leathers, shoes, leather breeches, bottle, bridle-thongs, flask and budgets, leather neck-pieces, spur-leathers, halters, bags and pouches, and nobody would wish to go through the winter without my craft."

In that list are probably found just about all of the uses of leather at that time.

Authentic evidence such as pieces of leather with silver ornaments attached to them exist in museums today, and are definitely identified as part of Saxon drinking cups. These were discovered in England in 1848.

And to go back further than that for a moment, the dry desert sands of Egypt, China, Turkey and other arid locations reveal examples of perfectly preserved leather articles that were in use as far back as 5000 B.C.

Egyptian writings tell us of the fine, soft leathers produced by the tanners of "The Old Kingdom", as that period from the 3rd – 6th dynasties is called. Leather in bright, gay colours was used to cover stools, chairs, beds, cushions, and to furnish canopies as early as 2980 B.C.

Although tanning processes were known prior to 1300 B.C., leather was not always tanned by the Egyptians, which might give rise to the thought that tanning was rather expensive. At the opening of the tomb of Tut-Ankh-Amen in 1924-25, Mr. Howard Carter, noted Egyptologist reports the finding of many leather articles belonging to that boy king. The horse trappings found with four chariots are reported to have been made of untanned leather. Despite the lack of tanning, the harnesses offer some of the earliest attempts of man to decorate leather. These harnesses had been covered with layers of gold. The manner in which the ancient Egyptian craftsmen applied the gold is not known, however it is not impossible that a modelling tool was used in much the same manner that our modern craftsmen use this tool. Should this theory prove to be correct, the modelling tool then becomes one of the most ancient tools still employed by the craft. The leather portions of these harnesses were reduced to a black, glue like mass, however, the gold coverings enabled modern craftsmen to reproduce the originals, and the gold has been placed onto the reproductions for display purposes.

Other leather items found in the tomb were a pair of slippers belonging to the king, and a leather covered seat stool. These articles were subsequently submitted to Dr. R. H. Pickard of the British Leather Manufacturers Museum for chemical analysis. After chemical analysis and examination, Dr. Pickard reported the stool cover to undoubtedly have been the skin of a goat. Due to the condition of the sandals, Dr. Pickard could not give a definite answer, but reported that they had probably been made of calfskin.

More recent excavations in Egypt have given us more history of the craft. A leather scroll inscribed with laws enacted in 1350 B.C. is of interest to the serious leather artisan. This law provided for the penalty of anyone convicted of stealing hides from the herdsmen of the Pharaoh's loan herds. These herds were owned by the king, but were tended by independent farmers. Any person convicted of stealing hide from these herdsmen would receive 100 blows, 5 of which must open wounds on the body, and the stolen hides would be confiscated by the soldiers. The ironic point of this law is the fact the soldiers were the ones most often convicted of stealing the hides.

The stone upon which Sesostris I inscribed the dedicatory history of the building of the Temple of Re, has long since perished. However, a scribe's practise copy of this inscription on a leather scroll was found in a corner of the temple some 500 years after the temple had been built. This scroll still exists and may be seen in the Berlin Museum. This temple was built during the 12th Dynasty.

Leather has a part in history during the reign of Thutmose III, when Thaneni recorded the first campaign during the seige of Megiddo. He recorded this campaign on rolls of leather. Unfortunately, these leather rolls, known by historians as the Thaneni Rolls, have returned to dust.

But the Egyptians were not the only ones to write historical events on leather, because early in the 12 century in Iceland, they started to write the sagas of the people and country. Those writings were mostly done on calfskin and with calf-blood. A few pieces of these writings still exist in museums.

Perhaps the most well-known period in the history of leathercraft is a period that might be called the Cordovan period. Historically, this period starts in 711 A.D. when the Saracens or Moors invaded Spain. One of the first places to fall into the hands of the invaders was that medieval city of culture, Cordova. It has been said of Cordova that it is the "soul" of Spain.

But Cordova means more than the city. Any

good dictionary will tell you what cordovan is: a Spanish leather made of goat-skin tanned and dressed, or later, of split horse-hides. Much used for shoes, etc, by the wealthy during the Middle Ages (Oxford Universal Dictionary) But not even encyclopedias give the history of cordovan or tell of the way in which it spread over the world. Neither do they tell of the wonderful art work that accompanied the leather itself and which is as important as the material known as cordovan.

The romance of cordovan leather leads one far back in time, back to the Middle Ages, when this kind of leather seems to have come into being. It takes us back to days when the Moors held Spain and when the city of Cordova was the cultural capital of the western world. During this period, the tenth century, London and Paris had streets of mud, no public lighting of any kind, and a garbage disposal system that consisted of pigs turned into the streets to clean up the filth. Not so in Moslem Spain. Not so in Cordova.

Tenth-century Cordova was a fabulous place. It ranked with Baghdad and Constantinople in the triad of the great capitals. According to Arabian historians, the city at the height of its splendor contained 1 000 000 inhabitants, 200 000 houses, 600 mosques, a library with 600 000 volumes, and 700 public baths.

It had miles of paved streets, lighted at night by lanterns. It had a mosque so large that even today only one has been built that outstripped it in size. And it had 1300 workers in the famous leather, as well as nearly the same number of artisans who worked in the weaving of silk and wool and who produced a kind of silken cloth encrusted with jewels.

Before we go any further, let it be said here and understood that the art of cordovan did not die with the Cordovan Moors. It survives to this day, and survives in the city of its birth, in Cordova on the banks of the Guadilquivir. And of course, it was carried from Cordova in the days of the city's decline. But to discuss this is to jump ahead too fast in our study.

The Moors left little in the way of the history of their famous leather. But some objects of art made of this material have survived from Moorish times. In museums in Cordova, in Madrid, Seville, London, Paris and New York one can see small chests covered with cordovan and embossed and tooled as the work was done by the original craftsmen. And the accounts, histories, romances, and sketches of many peoples in Europe and in the East speak of this famous leather.

From Russia to Glasgow, from Norway to Sicily the leather was known and coveted. Men paid fabulous prices for it, and there was never enough to fill the many demands. It was truly the leather of royalty. It was turned out by guilds of highly trained Moorish specialists and the techniques used by them were so exacting and the premium for good work set so high that not many imitations appeared. The only people who were able to approach the excellence of true cordovan were the Moors of Morocco. At some time during the glory of Cordova, Moroccan Moors came to the great city to learn the craft. We do not know who these men were, nor even if they intended to stay and make a living or to return with the techniques they had learned. But return to Morocco they did, and it was not long until the Moroccan leather industry began to flourish and even to rival that of Cordova. The techniques were very similar, of course. Both cordovan and morocco were fine-grained, soft coloured leather, chiefly made of goat-skins, and later of split horse-hides – the splitting was done to retain the grain of the heavier leather –; both were dyed on the outer or grain surface with some colour; both were finished in a peculiar ribbed or rough granulated surface by means of an engraved boxwood ball.

With such a history why did cordovan leather almost cease to exist in Spain?

What cut it off in its full flower and left only one small factory surviving in modern Cordova? That is another story, and a long one, but the essential facts can be quickly given. Cordova was conquered and was taken away from the Moors in the thirteenth century by King Ferdinand III, known as the Saint. King Ferdinand did not stifle Moorish art in the city. He even encouraged it. It was not until later, until the year 1492 that the end of Moorish Spain came. Ferdinand and Isabella, after a long and terrible war with the King of Granada, took that city in January. Part of their plan of conquest and of the re-unification of their country called for the expulsion of all peoples of non-Christian religious beliefs. First they drove out the Jews. Thousands upon thousands of these people were given the choice of leaving Spain or of accepting conversion to Christianity. We know that some worshipped Allah even after this, but always in the greatest secrecy, for the Inquisition was active and ever watchful. The penalty for those who had once become Christians and who returned to their own faith was death at the stake. Some burned others finally forgot their Moslem faith. At last all traces of Islam had been stamped out. The Moors left in Cordova, the ones who practised the ancient leather craft, today are good Catholics, but in their faces one sees the same features he sees in Algiers and Tunis. The mark of the Moor is still in them. And from generation to generation for hundreds of years they have passed down from father to son the techniques of making cordovan leather. They belong to one clan, or are at least trained and hired by one clan. There is only one factory in Spain that produces real cordovan and only one store that sells it. It is true folk-craft and there is nothing quite like it any place else in the world.

Tourists to Cordova may remember the attractive shop or display room in the old portion of the city, in the Moorish market place known as the Zoco. It is called Meryan and is known all over Spain and Portugal as the home of genuine and fine cordovan ware. The Meryan factory will make on order almost anything that can be made of leather. Their prices are high, from a Spanish viewpoint, and only Spaniards who are well-off can patronize the shop.

And there is much to buy. The leather panel with the herd of deer measures nearly six feet and is made of fine horse-hide. It was made as the facing for a door. The lady's purse is, of course, modern in design, but the art work is very ancient and preserves a pattern of Moorish origin, seen in Spanish tiles and other ceramics. The cover for a chair seat looks very Moorish, and may be an ancient design also.

Meryan makes leather wall hangings, some as large as tapestries, folding screens, chair backs and seats, covers for whole chairs and sofas, leather chests of many sizes, some square or oblong, some round or cylindrical, leather wainscots and friezes, decorative shields, and a number of other useful and decorative objects.

From the time King Ferdinand III conquered Cordova until the end of Moorish Spain in 1492 the Moors spread all over Europe. Every nation on the continent learned the Cordovan techniques of decorating leather. In time they came to perfect their own techniques, but to this day, all leather work shows at least a small amount of Cordovan influence.

The French, Italian and Dutch were the most dedicated leather artists on the entire continent. Many very fine examples of their work are on display in the Cluny Museum in France. The following is a partial list of the leather exhibited there:

Caskets and writing cases of repousse or chase leather of the 14th century are examples of Spanish craftsmen. Two of the earliest examples of leather work that have no functional purpose are exhibited as the work of 15th and 16th century Italian artists. The first of these is a decorative panel depicting The Madonna. The latter work is an engraving (carving), which shows the Flight of Aeneas.

One piece of work that has created a great deal of interest with our modern leather crafters is a Spanish trunk, probably of a period between the 16th and 17th centuries. This trunk is of leather, but the decoration has been embroidered onto the leather.

A shield belonging to some fallen Palmyrene archer was discovered near Damascus in 1924. This ancient warrior seems to have broken with the technique of his contemporaries in that he used colour alone to decorate his shield.

Certainly it would be interesting to contemplate the "might have beens" and the "probablys" surrounding this unknown soldier, but we must put aside this temptation. We could spend considerable time dreaming that this man was truly an artist, that he had the courage to break from tradition and employ his own artistic dictates. Beyond a doubt, he was a man of education, that his shield was a map of his travels, complete with the intervening mileages.

Few men, if any, had sufficient education to perform such a feat in his day, certainly never a common archer.

If the French, Italian and Dutch were the most dedicated leather artists on the continent, the English were not far behind.

During the troubled reigns of the Lancastrian and Yorkist kings, London remained peaceful and considerably increased in wealth. The government of London was conducted by members of the great merchant companies, who whatever their names might suggest (goldsmiths, leathersellers, fishmongers and so on) dabbled in many kinds of commerce of which their chief profits came from exports. As the original smaller craft guilds disappeared such strong English bodies as the London Livery Companies grew.

These companies had legal incorporation power

to hold land and were governed by a select body called the Court of Assistants, whose members reached office undemocratically by virtue of their swollen moneybags.

According to the second Report of Municipal Corporations' Commissioners 1837, each Livery Company was given an order of precedence, of which there are eighty-four still in existence.

Ranking fifteenth in order of precedence, The Worshipful Company of Leathersellers, was granted its charter of Incorporation in the year 1444. There is evidence, however that organized leathersellers were working in England from the early 1200's for records show the existence of a "Fraternity of Tanners and White Tawyers".

From this early date the leatherworkers seem to have established themselves at the north side of the City of London where a good supply of water was to be found.

It appears that the Leathersellers' Company was a successor of two earlier fraternities, the "Gray Tawyers" (tanners), and "Whittawyers" (white tanners). Existing in the thirteenth century, these two brotherhoods were important enough to acquire, Ordinances and By-Laws to govern their own craft. A mutual protection circle was thus formed which also included the Pelterers and Skinners - the men who flayed the carcasses.

In 1372 during the reign of King Edward III, it appears from the records written in Norman French, that the Leathersellers were worried about the prostitution of their craft. And on this date, together with Craft of Pursers, presented to the Court of Aldermen, a Bill to bring in stringent regulations to stop fraudulent dealings in dyeing and staining inferior leather by charlatans. The Bill was granted, and four Supervisors of the trade were appointed.

More "Articles" and "Ordinances" followed and fines from around 90 cents (more than a month's salary in those days) were imposed on "rebellious" masters and servants who would not conform to the rules of the craft.

King Henry VI granted the Leathersellers their Charter of Incorporation, and the Wardens of the Company were given powers covering the whole of England to regulate and ensure the high quality of craftsmanship.

Further Charters were granted to the Leathersellers down the ages and today the Company maintains a close connection with the industry it represents and continues to support its interests and to preserve the traditions of the craft.

This is particularly seen in the activities of the Company in the field of technological education. In 1951 the Leathersellers' Technical College in Bermondsey, London, was reestablished as the National Leathersellers College. It is now completely re-equipped and considered to be one of the most up-to-date tanning schools in the world. Here, and in many other Colleges of Handicraft throughout Great Britain, the ancient handcraft of decorating leather is taught, of which the following may be noted.

TOOLING, or FLAT MODELLING. The simplest of decoration, the design being traced, outlined or tooled with a steel tracer on a glass or marble surface. The background is pressed as flat as possible, or punched with a matting or other punch.

EMBOSSED LEATHERWORK. This most popular method, also called LEATHER REPOUSSE, raises the design from the back to bring it into relief, which is then filled to keep the raised part in place.

SURFACE MODELLING. A modelling on plastic paste.

CUT or INCISED LEATHER. This most artistic method of design is cut in by means of a special knife; the incision being opened with the tracer or opener, and one side pressed back with the modeller into the background.

CARVED LEATHERWORK. This is really embossed cut-work, where the portions of the design are cut inwards with a lancet, then the upper portion of the leather raised with a ballended tool.

Other arts are HAMMERED LEATHER, or BLIND TOOLING, PUNCHED LEATHERWORK, VENETIAN LACQUER, STENCILLING on LEATHER, LEATHER APPLIQUE, POKER-WORK, LAMELLE (decoration by means of metal strips, or thongs), RACINAGE, or MARBELLING, LEATHER MOZAIC and so on.

The Leathersellers' Company endow other schools, and supervise and endow houses and apartments for senior citizens.

As long as the Leathersellers' Company exists steps will be taken to ensure that the high quality of British leather goods is maintained. In a world where the old hand-crafts are slowly disappearing this Company is fighting a winning battle to defend their reputation of 500 years.

If you think that there is money in leathercraft today you are right; but you should have been around a few centuries ago.

There was not only money in leather in those days but there was also money made of leather. That's right! As recently as 1574 leather coins were issued and used during the Siege of Leyden. Before and since that time, leather has been put to just about every other use imaginable.

And to think that it has taken modern man so long to discover the craft as a hobby - and to realize the satisfaction that there is in working in leathercraft.

However, judging from the advancement and rapidly growing popularity of the craft, we are making up for lost time.

Leathercraft may have been a rather crudely executed vocation in the primitive times. There is no doubt however that a foundation was laid which advanced very noticeably in the middle ages and continued to improve, as a craft, up to the present.

Written history tells us that one of the first methods used in working leather was known as "cuir bouilli". Translated "cuir" means leather and "bouilli" means boil. As "boiled leather" the term was used to describe a method of moulding and hardening leather.

The origin of the term could have been the practice, then commonly used, of "boiling" the leather. This was done by making a leather vessel, filling it with water, then dropping very hot rocks into the water until the water was boiling. Then the water was poured out and the leather was moulded into any desired shape while it was still soft. The method was used to mould such articles as shields, helmets, knee-caps, leather bottles and drinking cups. There was also a shirt-like garment that would compare with our present-day bullet-proof vest and other medieval armour for man and his horse.

It should be noted that through all the ages this method has played a very important part in the craft. It exploits the combined strength and suppleness of good leather.

In some treatments in addition to the procedure already mentioned, resin, or a mixture of wax and resins, was used on the leather goods. In fact, today this is still done in the manufacturing of certain types of pump cups which are moulded on metal dies, immersed in molten wax and then put back on the dies.

The basic process was a fore-runner of the method used today in manufacturing leather trunk and suit-case corners, scabbards, cases for surveyor's tapes, some saddle seats and motorcycle or bicycle seats and small leather boxes and cases.

In this method the vegetable tanned leather is left in cold water until all the fibres are thoroughly soaked and softened. Then the leather is completely drained of water and is then shaped and moulded into any desired shape and ornamented by modelling tooling, carving and punching.

The Saxon drinking cup, previously mentioned, showed a highly developed technique that was used on smaller articles. For larger pieces, history written of the fourteenth century tells of Edwards III's troops carrying small boats of "cuir bouilli" into France.

While the earliest surviving examples of leather

water bottles date from about the fifteenth century. There is a record that a "guild of leather bottlers" existed in London in 1873 and it is believed that leather bottles were made as early as the eleventh century.

Shakespeare wrote in Henry VI, Part III, scene V, "cold thinne drink of this leather bottle."

Leather bottles appear in advertising written in the eighteenth century. Some of them were still in use in England around the turn of the last century. The wealthy had bottles which were richly ornamented and even those of the most humble were stamped with simple designs. The most popular and prominent decoration was the Fleur-de-Lis. One specimen exists today which had this imported motif all over the front of the bottle.

Another decorated bottle in a London museum, which was presumably used for ecclesiastical purposes, has the Sacred Heart and two initials carved on one side and a cross and the sacred letters, I.H.S. on the other side.

There is no doubt that these leather bottles were popular and plentiful in early England. They are constantly mentioned in literature, in song and stories and in inventories. One song, dating from at least the sixteenth century, is today a kind of theme song for the Worshipful Company of Leather-sellers in London.

One of the stanzas runs:
"I wish in Heaven his soul may dwell,
That first devised the leather bottle."

As a matter of fact, leather drinking-mugs were so large and so commonly used about 1635 that French visitors to England returned home to report that "the Englishmen drink out of their boots."

In those days glass and pottery were scarce and expensive and leather provided the utensils for all classes. The leather mug of the wealthy may have been lined with pewter and decorated with silver while the poor man's mug was lined with pitch but essentially they were all the same, in taverns, in homes and in the king's palace.

Even after pottery and glass became more common, the "black-jacks" - which the mugs were called - were still in use in many parts of England regularly until the latter part of the nineteenth century.

But in addition to these utensils, the travellers of those early days needed other things. They required bags and other sturdy containers to carry on their sometimes hazardous journeys.

Again leather was the answer. The leather craftsmen provided sheaths for daggers, scissors and knives, quivers for arrows, containers for flint, steel and tinder, power and shot and other items.

All of these were made of "cuir bouilli," light in weight and very tough. They were gracefully shaped and those of the wealthy were richly ornamented with punching, carving and were sometimes coloured and adorned with shining metal. Those of the poor were carved or stamped instead of being silver mounted.

It is known that as far back as the seventh century Saxon warriors wore leather jackets upon which metal discs were sewn to form an armored coat. And in a manuscript of the thirteenth century we learn that the weight of the metal armor so impeded the Saxon warriors, particularly when they were persuing the Welsh into the mountain country that leather armor replaced the heavy metal-studded garments.

Leather armor was made by sewing hard leather, probably "cuir bouilli," to a soft leather garment. These were sewn with pieces overlapping each other in a manner resembling the scales on a fish. As a decoration, two contrasting colours were often used. Leather helmets were commonly worn by the warriors.

During the period around 1300 and for several centuries afterwards, an important and popular leather was "buff-leather." This leather was originally the hide of the European buffalo, thereby deriving its name. The pale yellow that the leather had, no doubt, originated our present day designation of "buff" as a colour.

The process used was "oil-oxygenation" and the results were very similar to our chamois now made of sheep skin. Of course, the buffalo hide was of tougher texture and it is said that it would turn the point of a sword.

This "shamoying" process is described in Homer's Iliad in about 1200 B.C. - thirty one centuries ago.

The buff tunic was worn extensively during the entire seventeenth century and was the fore-runner of the popular doe-skin coat which was worn until late in the eighteenth century. Buff was also used to make gloves and gauntlets, including armored gauntlets with small steel plates on the back. Today, in the London museum there is an Elizabethan buff leather cone-shaped hat, arrayed with pink lining.

Leather girdles were another of the chief wares of the leather sellers of the twelfth century. Girdle makers were so numerous and so well organized that they formed a "Gild of Girdlemakers." Their organization was so powerful that they were able to impose fines on "unlicensed" girdle makers. Many of the girdles were richly ornamented with precious stones, metal, silk tassels and embroidery.

"Pouch makers" and "pursers" were also in prominence during the fourteenth century. They were probably the actual beginners of the craft of leather hand-bag makers which are numerous today.

They fashioned decorated pouches, purses and hand-bags for both sexes. There was a great variety of styles and designs. The quality of their workmanship was high. Their imagination created many styles and many forms of decoration including carving and stamping.

The woman's handbag was an important accessory then, as it is today. In medieval times there were two crafts devoted to the making of these necessities. The "pouch makers" first appear in history in 1327 and the "pursers" who are first mentioned, so far as we know, in manuscripts of 1372.

Information about these craftsmen is very scanty. They were absorbed by the "leathersellers" organization in about 1517. In ancient pictures examples of their work show that the designing and making of handbags, purses, pouches and wallets was a fine art in the fifteenth century. Perhaps strangely, many of the devices used today were in use then.

The embossing, modelling embroidering, folding, pleating, the ornamental stitching and the use of metal frames were not too unlike our craftsmanship of today.

In the history of leathercraft we first learn of saddle makers in about 1310. Ancient drawings show that not all saddles were made of leather but later illustrations do show beautifully ornamented saddles of doe-skin with much stitching and applique work.

As the craft advanced more guilds were organized and they, no doubt, did much to protect the craft. Records shows that saddle makers were severely punished if they produced bad work. In 1648 one saddler was fined for making "two noughtie straps." In 1608 another was not only fined for making a faulty saddle with "evil workmanship" but was also forced to witness the burning of the saddle in front of his shop.

We shall not go deeply into the very obvious use of leather as footwear, for that should come under the category of another craft - boot and shoe making - and an entire book could be written on the subject.

For example - there are twenty-eight known steps in the advancement of boot and shoe making up to the seventeenth century in England alone.

In America, of course, the Indians wore, and still wear moccasins. The earliest settlers wore boots and shoes which they brought with them from England. Among these settlers were cobblers who began to design and make footwear which was more suitable to the rough existence in the new country. Then came the woodsman's boots, hob-nailed shoes, dress shoes for the more genteel, then the cowboy boots, military boot and leather puttees.

And so, we come down to the present day footwear which includes just about every style and shape and every type of leather from snake and lizard skins to cordovan and shark skin.

For a long time, since the medieval days in England, the craft was a jealously guarded secret, with guilds actually organized with the crafts —

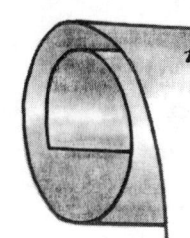

men passing the secrets of the craft only to their sons or to those who served long apprenticeships. Most often the fathers trained their sons in the craft and kept their secrets in the immediate family.

Fortunately leathercraft is no longer a secret. One man in particular is responsible for this, and indeed, no history of our craft, short or long, could be considered complete without some mention of this man. We, as leathercrafters, must forever pay tribute to Mr. F. O. BAIRD. Mr. Baird was one of the masters of the craft and saw the need of the people to have a craft which must be done by hand alone, also the need of the craft for the new concepts that the public would put into use. Since the time when Mr. Baird began teaching public classes in the mysteries of the craft, many others have formed ranks with him; far too many to list in this short space.

Such men, true artists, as Mr. ROBERT MUMA of Toronto, Canada; Mr. BERNARD WOOLF of Detroit, U.S.A.; and the king of all leather artists Mr. AL STOHLMAN.

Two men who must take their place in the history of the craft are Mr. RICHARD "DICK" McGAHAN and Mr. DAVE TANDY. These two men are the men most responsible for discovering ways to produce tools and almost foolproof patterns at a price that each and everyone of us can meet. Perhaps this more than any other advance in the craft will stand out in the years to come as the greatest achievement of man in the long history of this great and wonderful medium with which we work and play.

Swivel knife

Beveler

Pear shader

Camouflage

Veiner

Seeder

Background

Decorating cuts

USE OF THE BASIC TOOLS

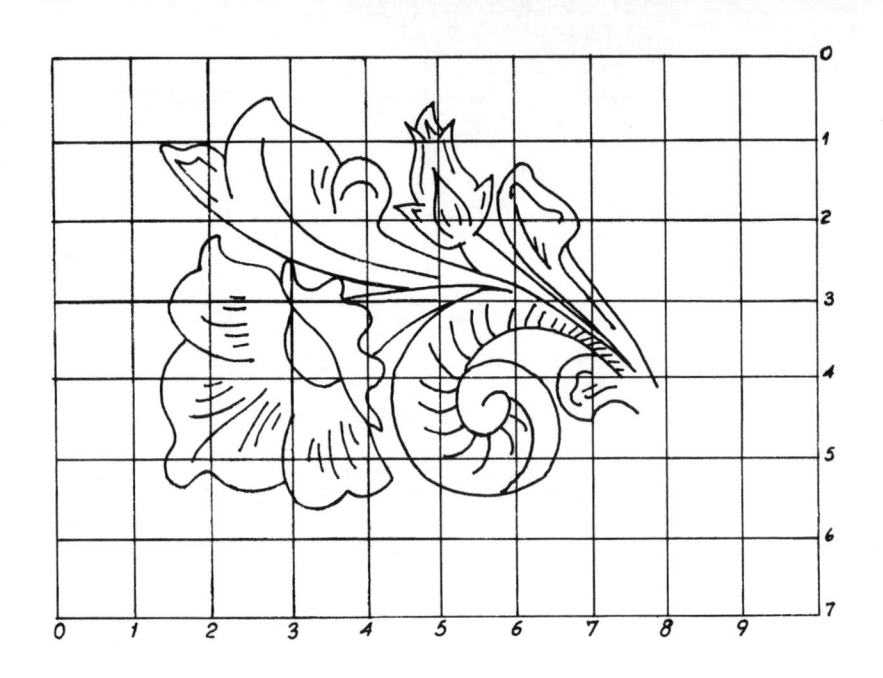

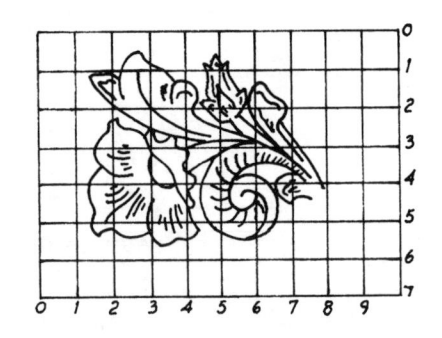

There is more than one way to reduce or enlarge a drawing. You can use a par graph, if you have one or the square method shown above, which I found to be even more effective. If you are working on a large drawing, it is good to have every fifth line each way in colour, preferably red, because that way it is much easier to work and less mistakes will be made. Another thing is if you are working on a very detailed part of the drawing you might have to make extra squares inside the already drawn squares, to locate more accurately all the finer details.

When you draw use light and dotted lines - which you darken later. Light lines are also easier to rub out if needed.

Like everything else, this needs practice to make perfect, and after some time you find it both an easy and quick method for reducing or enlarging designs. The first step is always to decide the sizes of the squares to use, both on the drawing you are working from and for the new size of the design. Always try to have each square in whole millimetres like if some design has to be halved, make one set of squares 10 mm and the others 5 mm.

It is good practice to have the lines for the squares on the back of tracing paper, so you won't rub them out if any rubbing out is done.

HOW TO REDUCE OR ENLARGE DESIGN.

Thickness of leather.	Used for.
1–2 oz. (0.4–0.8 mm)	Used for wallets, such as one-piece wallets and inside pockets, when carved. Also smaller articles.
2–3 oz. (0.8–1.2 mm)	Used also for wallet backs, pocket secretary, and zipper gussets. Also small projects.
3–4 oz. (1.2–1.6 mm)	Can be used for wallet backs, zipper gussets and where leather needs more body than comparable weight calfskin.
4–5 oz. (1.6–2.0 mm)	Intermediate weight, used for slightly heavier articles than above, or lighter than below.
5–6 oz. (2.0–2.4 mm)	For small bags, bag straps and some types of belts. Can be used for brief cases.
6–7 oz (2.4–2.8 mm)	Ideal for most carved handbags and bag straps, belts, such as contour belts or filigree work.
7–8 oz. (2.8–3.2 mm)	For many types of belts, large handbags, brief case backs and small pistol holders.
8–9 oz. (3.2–3.6 mm)	Ideal for wider belts, rifle holsters, pistol holsters, saddle bags and motorcycle belts.
9–10 oz. (3.6–4.0 mm)	Used primarily for heavy duty pistol holders and wider types of belts.
10–11 oz. (4.0–4.4 mm)	For belts, where strength and body is required, like lineman's belts.

LEATHER THICKNESS AND USE.

Style.	Edge distance. mm	Amount of lacing required.				
Running Stitch.	3	1½ x distance to be laced.				
	4.5	1½ x	"	"	"	"
	6	1½ x	"	"	"	"
Single Whip Stitch.	3	3½ x	"	"	"	"
	4.5	3¾ x	"	"	"	"
	6	4 x	"	"	"	"
Double Whip Stitch.	3	8¼ x	"	"	"	"
	4.5	10 x	"	"	"	"
	6	11 x	"	"	"	"
Cross Whip Stitch.	3	5 x	"	"	"	"
	4.5	6 x	"	"	"	"
	6	6¼ x	"	"	"	"
Single Loop Stitch.	3	6 x	"	"	"	"
	4.5	7 x	"	"	"	"
	6	8 x	"	"	"	"
Double Loop Stitch.	3	7½ x	"	"	"	"
	4.5	8¼ x	"	"	"	"
	6	9 x	"	"	"	"
Triple Loop Stitch.	3	9 x	"	"	"	"
	4.5	9½ x	"	"	"	"
	6	10 x	"	"	"	"
Mexican Basket Weave.	3	8½ x	"	"	"	"
	4.5	9 x	"	"	"	"
	6	9½ x	"	"	"	"

Note:

Add 10% to above formula for splicing and ending lacing.

FORMULA FOR STYLES OF EDGE LACING.